TAKE BACK YOUR LIFE

A WORKING MOM'S GUIDE TO WORK-LIFE BALANCE

TAKE BACK YOUR LIFE

A WORKING MOM'S GUIDE TO WORK-LIFE BALANCE

DR. LISA HERBERT

TAKE BACK YOUR LIFE
Published by Purposely Created Publishing Group™

Copyright © 2018 Lisa Herbert

All rights reserved.

No part of this book may be reproduced, distributed or transmitted in any form by any means, graphics, electronics, or mechanical, including photocopy, recording, taping, or by any information storage or retrieval system, without permission in writing from the publisher, except in the case of reprints in the context of reviews, quotes, or references.

Printed in the United States of America

ISBN: 978-1-947054-66-0

Special discounts are available on bulk quantity purchases by book clubs, associations and special interest groups.
For details email: sales@publishyourgift.com or call (888) 949-6228.
For information logon to: www.PublishYourGift.com

Dedication

This book is dedicated to the community of women who have uplifted and supported me: my mother, surrogate mothers, aunts, cousins, sister friends, coaches, mentors and spiritual partners. You all deserve to live a life of happiness, joy, peace and fulfillment; free of guilt about wanting to take time for yourself and feed your soul.

Table of Contents

Acknowledgments ix
Introduction 1

Chapter 1: The Reason Behind the Balance Movement....9
    What Is Work-Life Balance? 9
    Why Having Work-Life Balance Is Important........... 11
    How Do We Prevent Burnout? 13

Chapter 2: The Five Stages of Change 21
    The Five Stages of Change Necessary to Create a
    Balanced Life 21
    S.M.A.R.T. Goals 26
    Wheel of Work-Life Balance.. 31

Chapter 3: Achieving a Healthy Balance........................... 43
    Reclaiming Your Health 43
    Renewing Your Health 49
    Restoring Your Health 54

Chapter 4: Achieving Balance in Your Career................. 59
    Use Your Talents and Gifts.. 59
    Decide on Your Limits 60
    Develop an Identity Outside of Work 61
    Develop a Schedule.. 66

Chapter 5: How to Have Balance in Your
    Relationships 69
    Parenting 69
    Marriage Balance 75
    Nurture Your Friendships 79

Chapter 6: How to Achieve a Healthy Mental Balance.... 85
    What Is Stress? 86

Conclusion 97
References 100
About the Author 103

Acknowledgments

First and foremost, I would like to thank my Lord and Savior Jesus Christ for giving me the gift of healing, for speaking to me, and for encouraging me to deliver this message. Thank you for always being there for me, uplifting me, and giving me the strength and courage to persevere. You have answered my prayers on so many occasions. I am truly thankful and blessed to be your child.

Thank you to the women who have been a part of my journey and who keep breathing life into me when I'm depleted. You hold a piece of the puzzle that defines me and tells my story. Thank you for loving me unconditionally, for supporting me, for crying with me, pushing me beyond my comfort zone, and praising me so that I could live this dream and be this person. I want each of you to know that you matter. I encourage you to stay whole and to take care of yourselves so we can continue to pay it forward.

To my family, thank you for always supporting me. You have been my biggest cheerleaders, championing me to receive my medical degree. Family is the foundation on which our lives are built. Through family we learn values, morals and a sense of identity. For me, my family is not just my nuclear family but my extended family of grandparents, aunts, uncles, cousins, and community.

To my husband who is my rock, my soul mate, my life partner. We met in college and have been joined at the hip ever since. You believed in me and my dreams, and you supported me in achieving my goals. I could not imagine spending my life with anyone else. I look forward to our continued love story and journey. You are the glue that holds our family together. Thank you for being a wonderful, supportive spouse, a great friend, and an awesome dad.

To my children, my babies. Being a mother is my greatest accomplishment. I breathed life into two amazing human beings who have changed my life forever. You taught me how to love unconditionally. You're strong, confident, intelligent, caring young adults who bring me so much joy. You are the reason I wake up every morning and why I continue to work hard every day. You both have made me so proud. I could not have asked for better children to raise.

To my mother, who taught me so much about resiliency and strength. As a young child, I could not even imagine the obstacles you had to overcome and the challenges you faced. Raising two children is not easy and you did an exceptional job. Ma, you taught me what it means to be a mom, how to be supportive and nurturing, how to be the disciplinarian when needed, and how to enjoy all that life offers. Your love for community and helping others was contagious, and I am a better person for having been raised by you.

To my father, the first man in my life who I looked up to and who made me feel special. Daddy, your support is always felt. I appreciate everything that you have taught me about the ups and downs of life, having confidence in myself, and wanting the best for myself.

To my siblings, who each holds a special place in my heart. I see some of me in each of you and I treasure the time we spend together. Although distance separates us, the love is still felt from miles away. Thank you for being in my corner and for having my back. I love my nieces and nephews and look forward to creating more memories for years to come.

Introduction

"Be aware of wonder. Live a balanced life - learn some and think some and draw and paint and sing and dance and play and work every day some."

—Robert Fulgham, American author.

For me, being in balance was the driving force behind striving to be more joyful, present, and healthy as well as develop more meaningful relationships. Being a wife, mother and physician was at times very overwhelming. I realized that I was not making time for the things that mattered most to me. I was preaching to my patients about exercise, but not getting enough exercise myself. I was not partaking in the things I love like reading an enjoyable book, listening to my favorite tunes, meditating, and spending time with family and friends. What I realized was that I was no longer energized to do God's work. I wasn't fully living with purpose. I was not living the life I wanted— one of peace, bliss, contentment and fulfillment. The signs of discontentment were there, but I did not address them. I thought if I worked harder and tried to be everything to everyone, I would be fulfilled; but the situation only worsened. I started to become disconnected. My children and husband realized that I was not fully present. I loved my career, but I felt a shift in how I reacted to things. My decision to find balance was important for both me and my family. My goal was to find balance so that my loved ones felt validated, listened to, loved and important. I no longer wanted to sacrifice family for a demanding work schedule. I no longer wanted to deprive myself of self-care. I had to develop the first step to creating work-life balance, which was to decide what a balanced life looked like for me. Then, I assessed each area of my life to determine my level of satisfaction.

For me, a balanced life included having time for a consistent spiritual practice and for deepening my faith. I developed a deep understanding and trust in God from being raised in the church. I knew that even during challenging times, my faith would carry me through. I knew that God was guiding me despite how difficult the road seemed. As a young girl and through my early adulthood, recharging my spiritual tank provided me with the strength and answers I needed when faced with tough decisions or situations. Making time for this spiritual connection kept me balanced and allowed me to be resilient. I realized that I needed to get back to that space where my spiritual practice was a more consistent part of my daily routine.

Having a balanced life also meant taking the time for my personal well-being. It meant taking the time to care for me. As a medical professional, I was trained to be the ultimate caregiver, often at the expense of my own health. I know how important it is to keep your health in check; yet, I was not taking my own advice. This would mean taking time to exercise, restoring healthy eating habits, and getting adequate sleep. Without these healthy habits, I was putting myself at risk for diseases that were a part of my family history, like hypertension and diabetes. I was also depriving myself of the energy I needed to get through the day and be there for others.

With this revelation, I started to put the pieces together to seek balance in my life. The first thing I had to do was be honest and ask myself if I was living the life I dreamed of. Was I living with purpose? Were my relationships healthy? Was I taking time for myself and developing my own identity beyond the role defined by my profession? If I wanted to live in balance and harmony, I had to act. This included taking time for internal reflection and realizing that I needed help. So, I shared my story of wanting a change in my life with a close friend and she suggested hiring a life coach. At first, I didn't know what a life coach was or how one would help. My friend shared that the right professional coach could provide an outside perspective and serve as an accountability partner to make sure I reached my goals. My time spent with my coach involved some deep soul searching, learning to speak my truth, owning my feelings, and verbalizing my wants so that I could put an action plan into place. After several months, I was ready to change the trajectory of my life with the framework the coach had provided me.

* * *

I wrote this book for working moms who are ready to make the changes necessary to live the life they want; for women who constantly feel strapped for time and guilty about shortchanging someone or something. We think it's not possible to change the course of our lives because it's too overwhelming. We put it on the back burner thinking we'll get to it. We are often too tired to make a move and begin focusing on areas of our lives that need work. We end up waiting for change to happen, but it never does. Well, I am here to tell you that *you* are the change. You don't need to wait on anyone else. We must learn to let go of guilt and the idea of being perfect, and strategically work on developing the life we want.

Is having a balanced life important to you? Are you seeking more time with your loved ones? How about more time for self-care and meaningful work? If you answered yes to any of these questions, this book will show you how to discover the work-life balance that is meant for you. We will walk through the four areas of your life: health, relationships, career, and spirituality. You will develop an understanding of their importance and explore how to achieve fulfillment in each of these domains. *Now* is the time to start putting a plan in place to achieve the life you desire.

Take Back Your Life Quiz

Before you start reading this book, let's see where you are in terms of your work-life balance. Are you in need of a drastic change? Are you hanging on by a thread or are you in good balance? Take this quiz and find out. Answer true or false to each statement. Give yourself a '0' for each true response, and a '1' for each false response. Add up your points to reveal how you scored.

I have enough time to devote to family and friends
____True
____False

I have time to eat healthy most days and rarely eat fast food
____True
____False

I often have enough time in my schedule for 'me time'
____True
____False

Most of the time I am not stressed
____True
____False

I always use all my vacation and personal time
____True
____False

I have enough time in my schedule to exercise at least three times per week
____True
____False

I feel like my relationship with my family is not affected by my work
____True
____False

I have enough time to spend on things I love to do
____True
____False

I feel energized and well rested most of the time
____True
____False

I never have a hard time saying no
____True
____False

I hardly ever miss important family events due to work
____True
____False

I am free of guilt and don't feel like I have to be perfect
____True
____False

IF YOU SCORED:	
0-3	You have a healthy work-life balance. Reading this book will reinforce what you need to do to maintain that balance.
3-6	You could use some help with improving your work-life balance before it starts to overwhelm you. Read this book to start making the necessary changes.
> 6	Your work-life balance is out of control. You need to act now to take your life back. Read this book to evaluate your current work-life situation and develop your action plan today.

CHAPTER 1:

The Reason Behind the Balance Movement

"When you have balance in your life, work becomes an entirely different experience. There is a passion that moves you to a whole new level of fulfillment and gratitude, and that's when you can do your best... for yourself and for others."

—Cara Delevingne

The issue of work-life balance has been debated and discussed for many years. Some believe it's not attainable. Some question if work-life balance really exists. Others believe that balance can be achieved by dividing their time equally between work and personal responsibilities.

WHAT IS WORK-LIFE BALANCE?

The dictionary definition of balance is a condition in which different elements are equal or in the correct proportions. Imagine a juggler who must learn how to keep several objects moving in the air at the same time by manipulating and rearranging the objects so they don't fall. This juggling act is what some people experience daily—the act of trying to handle the demands and responsibilities of work and family. Every day, families struggle to make sure all areas of their lives are receiving the same amount of attention while simultaneously holding down very demanding jobs. This juggling act may be too much for some to handle.

Work-life balance is not having an equal share of time between your work and personal life. Work-life balance is individual and unique to each person and it can change based on the current needs of your responsibilities at work and home. We should look to achieve fulfillment in the different areas of our lives and to strive for a healthy mind, body, and spirit.

According to a June 2014 White House report titled *Nine Facts About American Families and Work*, 46% of working Americans said their job demands "sometimes or often" interfered with their family life. This figure increased from 41% in 2002.

According to a Harris Poll survey for Ernest & Young, managing work and family responsibilities is proving especially difficult for US Millennials. Seventy-eight percent of Millennials are nearly twice as likely to have a spouse/partner working at least full-time compared to 47 percent of Baby Boomers. Consequently, "finding time for me" is the most prevalent challenge faced by millennial parents who are managers in the US, followed by "getting enough sleep" and "managing personal and professional life." The Millennials are our next generation and unless we start to address this problem, we will have a generation of stressed, disconnected, burned-out adults who are not able to effectively contribute to their families, their careers, or to the progression of our nation as a whole. We will also have a generation of adults who are at greater risk for developing health issues such as heart disease, stroke, obesity, and mental health disorders like anxiety and depression.

WHY HAVING WORK-LIFE BALANCE IS IMPORTANT

"Being in control of your life and having realistic expectations about your day-to-day challenges are the keys to stress management, which is perhaps the most important ingredient to living a happy, healthy and rewarding life."

—Marilu Henner

Having work-life balance is important because if it is left unchecked, it can lead to burnout. Burnout is a type of chronic stress where there is physical, emotional and/or mental exhaustion. There are many causes of burnout such as working longer hours, having less time for family and social interactions, and increased personal demands. But burnout doesn't happen overnight. A series of events, stressors, and changes happen over time and build up to a point where you start to feel like you can't escape. If you're not paying attention to what's going on around you, by the time you become aware and address what's happening, it may be too late. Some warning signs of burnout are lack of enthusiasm about work, no longer having a positive outlook about work, feeling exhausted both mentally and physically, lack of empathy, thinking about quitting work or changing jobs, being easily irritated, and having trouble sleeping. How do we feel fulfilled in the different areas of our lives without feeling stressed and overwhelmed, even during times when work and life are very demanding? We need to identify what is important to us in our personal and professional lives and decide what takes priority when the struggle to be present for both arises. Being out of balance and living with burnout can cause you to miss life's most important moments. We can't be present for others without having our own physical and mental health in balance.

HOW DO WE PREVENT BURNOUT?

1) Learn to say NO

In this digital age, our portable devices allow us to be reached at all times. To reduce this accessibility, we need to set boundaries. By doing this, we not only say no to the things that do not serve us personally or professionally, but we also let others know how and when we want to be contacted. This frees up time in our schedules, which we can utilize however we see fit. As a working mom who wanted work-life balance, I realized that by always saying yes, I was becoming inundated with tasks that I could never complete. I had to learn that no is a complete sentence. As working moms, we are used to taking care of everyone else. That often means saying yes to things we don't have time for or that we don't want to do. Being able to firmly say no takes time. It may feel at first like you are being selfish, but in reality, you are simply creating boundaries and preventing yourself from being overbooked. You are protecting yourself from stress and burnout. Before you say yes, truly evaluate if it is something you can and are willing to accomplish. Protect yourself and your time.

Below is an example of a woman who has overextended herself.

Mary is a married mother of two who works as a director for a marketing company. Her children are four and eight. She often has to work long hours to meet project deadlines and cannot find time for herself or her family. When she is not working, she is attending to family responsibilities. She tries very hard to make every family function, but often has to miss out on important occasions. She does not see any way out of her current situation, so she continues down this daunting path of ignoring what's going on around her. Instead of reflecting on her thoughts and behaviors surrounding her current work-life balance situation, she works harder to try to make everyone happy by saying yes to every request. Due to her behavior, she spirals deeper and deeper into a state of resentment, which leads to stress, anxiety, and eventually burnout. Mary is giving up what she truly wants in life and not living out her dreams. Mary must learn when to say NO.

2) Adapt to change

Our personal and professional lives go through different stages. Just like we have to adapt to the changing four seasons, we also have to learn to adapt to the various stages in our personal and professional lives. There will be times when our personal lives may need more attention because of events such as: the birth of a child, the loss of a loved one, or illness. Our professional lives may also need more attention during times of increased work demands like: working on a new project, having to travel for work, learning new material, or increased work volume during certain times of the year. Being aware of what's important, being willing to be flexible, and developing a framework to know how you are going to deal with these challenges will help to make these encounters easier to manage and keep you in balance.

> *Let's look at Pauline. Pauline is the successful CEO of her own beauty business. She is married with three children. She recently learned that her mother was very ill. Her mother needs help going to doctor's appointments, grocery shopping, and cooking her meals. Pauline is the only sibling who lives close to her mother and finds herself solely taking on the responsibility of being her mother's caretaker. Pauline is starting to feel the pull between work, family life at home, and the responsibility of being a caregiver for her parent. This new change in Pauline's life has caused her own schedule and household responsibilities to shift. She must now find a way to make time for taking care of her mother as well as keeping up with her own responsibilities at work and home.*

Pauline needs to take time for internal reflection. She can start by finding a quiet space to unwind. Reflecting in a quiet space, free of distractions, allows new ideas and solutions to problems to emerge. In this quiet space, Pauline should look at where she is in her current work-life balance state. She should ask herself where she wants to be and what she needs to do to get there. What changes must be made to make her new situation work?

3) Ask for help

Sometimes as women, we feel that asking for help is somehow a sign of weakness. We feel that we should be responsible for everything that occurs in our family's lives and if we ask for help we are not living up to our potential. Over time, this behavior causes us to experience frustration, as it's impossible to carry out multiple tasks and responsibilities twenty-four hours a day, seven days a week. This burden can lead to increased tension and a strain on our relationships. Asking for help and seeking advice relieves some of the pressure of responsibility. It also allows us the freedom to carve out some time for ourselves so that we can be our best when called upon. Help can come from family members, friends, neighbors, or even coworkers. One of the best practices is to work on creating a village of people who you can call on in times of need. A recent study (conducted by Arizona State University and the Mayo Clinic) of working moms who are medical professionals found that they are more susceptible to stress and burnout because of their continuous role as a primary caregiver. This study also showed that these caregiving women can significantly reduce their feelings of burnout by participating in support groups at work. Mothers in other professions are often caregiving women as well. We are not only taking care of child related responsibilities, but we are often the caregivers for our aging parents. Support groups at work or in your community can provide you with a safe space to discuss your struggles as well as offer camaraderie among other women having the same experiences.

> *Pauline, in the scenario above, could find a support group of other caregivers or form one of her own, to help her get through this challenging time of being primary caregiver to her aging parent. She shouldn't attempt to manage this on her own. She can also ask for support from her family members, friends, the healthcare community, and her job. She must be willing to ask for help and to let others help her. She must be willing to create boundaries and say no to taking on new roles and responsibilities that are of low importance.*

4) Recharge

Learning to take the time to recoup in between challenges is also important. Time is needed to recharge so that it's easier to be resilient and bounce back. Recharging allows your mind to develop a new set-point. You will become more focused, more productive, and better prepared to deal with the next challenge that comes your way. Learning to say the word no also frees up time for yourself. When we take time to recharge, we can be fully present for those who depend on us. When we take time to recharge, we lessen the chances of becoming overwhelmed and stressed. Chronic stress develops because we allow negative situations to continue to build without taking time to reset. It's difficult to sustain living with constant stress. So, taking ten minutes a day to sit quietly can have long-lasting effects, allowing us to become better versions of ourselves. We must create the lives we want to live.

What would have to be true for that to happen? What would you have to let go of? What areas of your life do you want to improve?

Take time to reflect on the above questions and write your responses below.

Take Back Your Life

CHAPTER 2:

The Five Stages of Change

"Progress is impossible without change, and those who cannot change their minds cannot change anything."

—George Bernard Shaw

THE FIVE STAGES OF CHANGE NECESSARY TO CREATE A BALANCED LIFE

The first step to creating your balanced life is deciding where you are in the process. As working women, we know how important work-life balance is. We often imagine what that life would look like. We hope for equal time spent between work and life, but we know that this is next to impossible; so, we never devote the time and energy to make the necessary changes. We never take the first step to create the life we so desperately want. Instead, we are left with goals that never get accomplished, dreams that never get fulfilled and relationships that never flourish. We continue in survival mode. Unless someone or something pushes us to make a change, our lives remain the same. Moving toward a balanced life requires a change in your behavior that develops over time. Just like a behavioral change to quit smoking or to start leading a healthy lifestyle takes time, it also takes time to start designing the life you want to live. Studies show that most people move through a series of stages when changing their behavior. The Stages of Change Model was developed by researchers Prochaska and DiClemente. The stages are:

Stage One: PRECONTEMPLATION

People in this stage are not ready to change a behavior and usually are not thinking about making a change in the future. They are aware a change must be made, but they are not ready to commit to a process to make it happen. It is the belief that people in this stage don't have the necessary information or resources to help them see what the outcome of changing their behavior will be. They also do not seek out the information necessary to make the change to their current situation, so they remain in the dark and don't ask for help. It is believed that people in this stage lack self-awareness. Self-awareness is your ability to understand how you perceive your current situation, how you react to problems, and how you respond to people when conflicts arise. It is also the ability to recognize how others view you. In the case of identifying if your work-life situation is in need of a change, you must be able to identify when work and personal responsibilities start to conflict with each other and then decide what has to change in order to improve the current state.

For example, let's say your work constantly interferes with your ability to attend your child's soccer games. You want desperately to attend, but instead of asking for time off or an adjustment to your work schedule, you become angry each time you can't go. This anger continues to build, leads you to become argumentative at home, and you start to act out at work. This constant conflict will only lead to increased stress overtime because you never address the situation. You walk around not realizing how much this is really affecting you and your family. You start to resent work. It's not that you no longer like your job, you just don't like the situation that your job is putting you in. Instead of identifying the challenge and addressing it, you ignore it. This makes you more likely to get stuck in this situation, which can lead to resentment and burnout. Increasing your level of self-awareness allows you to reflect on your situation, instead of ignoring it. Self-awareness allows you to examine how you are reacting to the perceived threat and start to develop a plan. Instead of holding on to resentment and anger, you become aware of these emotions and develop a course of action to make changes to your behavior. If you can't see where you currently are in life and measure how it is affecting you, you can't design an action plan to improve it.

Stage Two: CONTEMPLATION

People in this stage are planning on making a change in the near future. They are aware of their current situation and realize that changing their behavior will bring about positive change. On the flipside, they are also very aware of the negative effects of changing their behavior. This often produces conflict and will cause some people to remain in this stage for a very long time. It is called **procrastination**. Think about an area in your life where you put off doing something. What was the reason you held off on making the necessary changes? Was it fear?

What leads a person to move out of this stage is usually the realization that changing the behavior will gain them something in return. For example, let's look at a person who smokes. What will that person gain from quitting? A person in this situation might say, "Quitting smoking will allow me to not only reduce my risk of lung cancer, but I will also be able to run around with my children because my breathing has improved." Let's also look at the example of not being able to take time off to attend your child's soccer game. Moving to the stage of contemplation requires taking the time to examine what is preventing you from being able to attend your child's event. What will you gain from developing a plan that allows you to spend more time with your child? At this stage, you should start to realize the positive changes that can be made with a new plan. These positive changes will include the ability to spend more time with your children. You may also recognize the possible negative outcomes of this change such as having to approach your boss. This may bring anxiety as you may not want to impose on another person nor do you want it to appear that you cannot handle your work and family responsibilities. You may have the urge to procrastinate to avoid the negative effects that could develop from making this change. However, you must realize that the positive effect of spending more time with your children far outweighs the internal fear that arises from speaking the truth. This stage allows you to release this resentment.

Stage Three: PREPARATION

People in this stage are ready to make a change in the immediate future. They have an action plan. For example, someone who is trying to quit smoking will talk with their physician and plan to set a quit date. They will ask for help from their family and friends regarding this behavior change. Having an action plan shows that you are serious about making changes.

Let's look back at the work-life example. You are encountering some new work demands, which is causing you to miss out on your children's activities. We stated earlier, that first you must learn how to adapt to change. In the previous section, we stated that you must first reflect on your current situation and write down what you want. Next, you must decide what is important to you. After a period of reflection, you must decide what you are willing to be flexible with in order to attend your children's activities. What will you have to change or get rid of to make this happen? How can you become flexible with your work schedule to still meet the demands of work and be there for your children? Who can you call upon to help you with this new schedule? What do you need to verbalize to your spouse and boss? This will become your plan. Once you have this process down, you can apply these steps to any new challenges that may come your way in the future.

S.M.A.R.T. GOALS

After you have decided on the change you would like to make to improve your work-life balance and you are preparing your action plan, make sure that you set **S.M.A.R.T.** goals. **S.M.A.R.T.** is an acronym for **S**pecific, **M**easurable, **A**chievable, **R**elevant and **T**imebound.

Setting S.M.A.R.T. goals provides you with a better chance of achieving the goals you set forth because you have clarified what you want, you are specific, and you have set a time frame for reaching your mark.

For example, if your goal is to have more time to attend your children's functions, your S.M.A.R.T. goal may look like the following:

- **SPECIFIC**

A specific goal is one that is clearly defined. Here you want to answer the Three W's: **What, Who, and Why**. The What is stating what your goal is. The Who is the person who benefits from setting this goal. The Why is the reason you are setting this goal and why it is important. An example of a specific goal may be:

What: "I want to achieve better work-life balance that allows me to spend more time attending my children's functions."

Who: "Not being able to attend their functions makes me feel stressed, causes me to resent work, and puts a strain on my relationship with my children."

Why: "Being there for my children's functions is important to me because I don't want to miss out on their formative years. My presence also lets my children know that I support them."

- **MEASURABLE**

Here you want to have a sense of the progress you are making. How will you know that you achieved your goal?

For example, "Creating the ideal work-life balance will require help from my family and work. It will require me to seek resources to help me achieve this goal. I'd like to be able to have time to attend x number of functions per month within the next three months."

- **ACHIEVABLE**

How can I accomplish this goal? How realistic is the goal you are setting for yourself? Do you have the resources to help you? Look at the goal you set above and determine if this goal is something that you can accomplish. Start to look at the resources you will need to help you. Maybe you need more help from your spouse with household duties. Maybe you can develop a list of friends, relatives and neighbors who can share with pickup and drop off; allowing you to stay a little longer at work some days to complete your tasks. Then you will still have that extra time to take off when needed. You should identify your support group and what changes you can make to your schedule.

- **RELEVANT**

How much does this goal matter to you? Is it worthwhile? Here is an example of what a relevant statement may look like: "Improving my work-life balance is important to me because it will lead to improved health, stronger relationships, and personal satisfaction."

- **TIMEBOUND**

When do you want to reach this goal? By setting a target date you give yourself a timeline to work with and reaching this goal becomes a priority. What do you need to do today, tomorrow, next week, and next month? A time bound statement may be, "In order to achieve work-life balance and have time to attend my children's functions, today I need to look at my job responsibilities and see where I can make adjustments. Next week I will…" "By next month I will…" And, by the third month I will have achieved…"

Stage Four: ACTION

People in this stage have made significant changes in the past six months. In this stage, you are putting your plan to action and seeing some positive results. You should have developed a list of close relatives and friends who are assisting you when you need help. You should have also developed a plan that allows you to be flexible when there is a change in your work or personal schedule. In this stage, it is important to remember that your action plan can always be tweaked, as circumstances will arise that call for you to make a shift in your plans. The key point here is to have developed self-awareness. Be willing to make the change because you have identified the positive effects of this adjustment and put a plan into action.

Stage Five: MAINTENANCE

People in this stage have made changes and are working to prevent reverting back to their previous behavior. They are very confident that they will continue to progress and work hard to maintain their new work-life balance transformation. They also know that if they go back to their previous habits they can revisit their action plan to fit their current situation.

Using the information above, assess how you currently prioritize your time in every area of your life. The "Wheel of Work-Life Balance" below provides some areas to look at: work, family and friends, spouse/partner, health, spiritual well-being, leisure, finances, and community service. Now, think about how you would like to prioritize your time to bring you the most fulfillment. On a scale of 1-10, with 1 being very dissatisfied and 10 being very satisfied, determine what your level of satisfaction is in every area of your life. Write the number in the corresponding slice of the wheel for each category. Next, identify the lowest number you will be satisfied with. Once you identify this number—let's say it's an eight—you may want to address the areas that rank less than eight.

WHEEL OF WORK-LIFE BALANCE

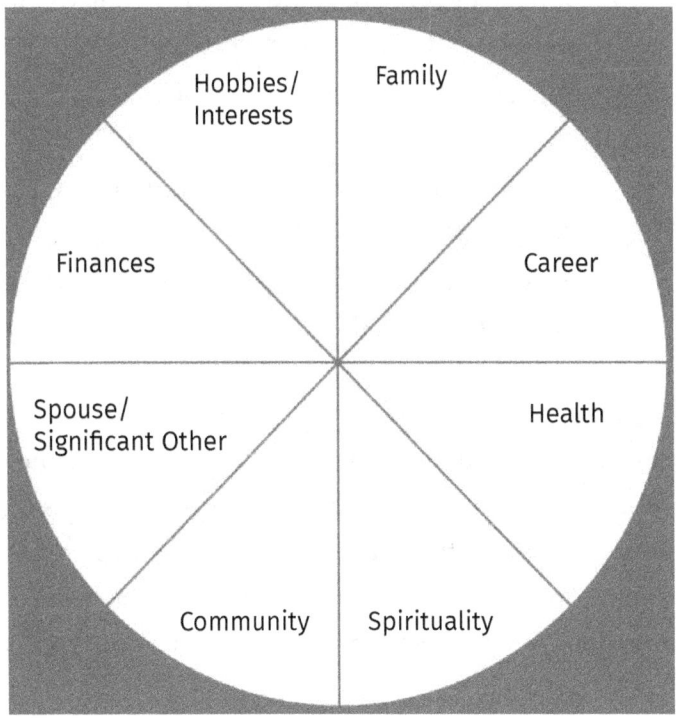

- How did you feel after completing this wheel?
- How do you feel about your current work-life balance situation as you look at your wheel?
- What should each of these areas look like for you to be in balance?
- How would you like to prioritize these areas differently?
- How would you like to spend time in each of these areas?
- Which areas are the most important for you to work on and improve immediately?
- What would you have to let go of to make these changes happen?
- Can you make these changes on your own or are you going to need help?
- Who can you count on to help you make these necessary changes?

Now that you have identified the most important areas that you need to address, use The Stages of Change Model to guide you to making the necessary changes on your own. Don't try to take on more than one area at a time. You don't want to become more overwhelmed, which will only halt your progress. Decide which area is most important to start with. After accomplishing one area move on to the next one.

WORKBOOK

Put your thoughts down below or in a journal. Ask yourself where you want to be and what you need to do to get there. How much better will your life be if you make these changes? What obstacles will you face in making these changes and how will you get over them?

First Area of Your Life:

_____

What Stage are you in?
Precontemplation or Contemplation?

Remember: If you are still in the Precontemplation Stage, you must do some internal reflection.

If you are in the Contemplation Stage and know that you must make a change, start to explore how changing the behavior will gain you something positive in return. What is the positive outcome? What possible negative effects of this change are you avoiding that are causing procrastination?

_____

_____

_____

_____

What is your goal in this area? Develop your goal into a S.M.A.R.T. goal.

Specific

_____

_____

_____

_____

Measurable

_____

_____

_____

_____

Achievable

_____

_____

_____

_____

Relevant

_____

_____

_____

_____

Timebound

_____

_____

_____

_____

Put your goal into action. Write the steps here.

_____

_____

_____

_____

Second Area of Your Life:

_____

What Stage are you in?
Precontemplation or Contemplation?

Remember: If you are still in the Precontemplation Stage, you must do some internal reflection.

If you are in the Contemplation Stage and know that you must make a change, start to explore how changing the behavior will gain you something positive in return. What is the positive outcome? What possible negative effects of this change are you avoiding that are causing procrastination?

_____

_____

_____

_____

What is your goal in this area? Develop your goal into a S.M.A.R.T. goal.

Specific

_____

_____

_____

_____

Measurable

_____

_____

_____

_____

Achievable

_____

_____

_____

_____

Relevant

___

___

___

___

Timebound

___

___

___

___

Put your goal into action. Write the steps here.

___

___

___

___

___

Third Area of Your Life:

_____

What Stage are you in?
Precontemplation or Contemplation?

Remember: If you are still in the Precontemplation Stage, you must do some internal reflection. If you are in the Contemplation Stage and know that you must make a change, start to explore how changing the behavior will gain you something positive in return. What is the positive outcome? What possible negative effects of this change are you avoiding that are causing procrastination?

_____

_____

_____

_____

What is your goal in this area? Develop your goal into a S.M.A.R.T. goal.

Specific

_____

_____

_____

_____

Measurable

_____

_____

_____

_____

Achievable

_____

_____

_____

_____

Relevant

___

___

___

___

Timebound

___

___

___

___

Put your goal into action. Write the steps here.

___

___

___

___

CHAPTER 3:

Achieving a Healthy Balance

It's impossible to have a healthy lifestyle if you are out of balance with your work and personal responsibilities. If you are working long hours, it is unlikely that you are taking the time to eat healthy and exercise. These habits are putting you at risk of developing chronic diseases like obesity, diabetes, heart disease, and hypertension. Adopting a healthy lifestyle is at the core of being in balance. Maintaining balance is only strengthened by having good health. You can't take care of others without having your own health in order. In this chapter, we will examine how to achieve a healthy balance by following The Three R's: Reclaiming Your Health, Renewing Your Health, and Restoring Your Health.

RECLAIMING YOUR HEALTH

A healthy lifestyle is achieved by aligning the mental, spiritual, and physical connection. Without a healthy foundation, it becomes impossible to keep up with the demands of work and family responsibilities. Lack of exercise and an unhealthy diet can lead to constant fatigue, loss of energy, frequent infections, and low stamina; making it difficult to have the work-life fulfillment you desire. Good health is essential to achieving your goals. As you begin to develop balance in your life, you should bring back healthy habits and fitness into your routine to help reduce stress, maintain a healthy weight, and increase your energy level. Some basic recommendations are:

Exercise

How many times have you heard that exercise is good for your physical health? Exercise improves your health by enhancing your immune system, lowering your blood pressure, controlling your weight, releasing tension, and managing stress. There are also other benefits to exercise. According to the New York Times "Well" report, exercise may improve memory and the ability to perform skilled tasks by increasing production of a protein that stimulates nerve cell health. Studies also indicate that exercise may reduce the risk of breast cancer. Researchers from the American Cancer Society found that walking at least seven hours per week is associated with a 14% lower risk of developing breast cancer after menopause, compared to those who walked three hours or less per week. All great reasons to put your walking shoes on and develop a consistent exercise routine.

So how often should one exercise? The American Heart Association recommends 30 minutes per day, five times per week of moderate intensity aerobic activity or 25 minutes of vigorous aerobic activity at least three days per week combined with high intensity muscle strengthening activity at least two or more days per week. Seem like a lot? Don't worry—there is also a benefit from dividing the time into two or three segments of 10-15 minutes per day. So, no excuses, let's get moving!

Exercise Tips

- To get started with your exercise routine, make a specific plan of action to meet your health goals. For instance: "I will exercise three times per week for 30 minutes by walking on the treadmill." Here you identified how often, the length of time, and the exact exercise.

- Pencil it in on your calendar and keep track. By making an appointment with yourself to exercise, you are making it a priority and planning. This allows you to make changes to your schedule if unexpected events occur.

- Use variety in your exercise routine. Take yoga one day, go to the gym the next, walk another day. This keeps exercise fun and interesting. You are more likely to stick to an exercise routine if you enjoy it. You are also more likely to be consistent with an exercise routine if you do it with a friend. Below are some non-traditional activities that count as exercise:

- Gardening
- Swimming
- Dancing
- Tennis
- Golf

Hold yourself accountable for your exercise goals. Write in a journal and monitor your progress.

Healthy Eating

Watch the Salt

The American Heart Association identified six salty foods that could increase your risk for heart disease and stroke. The "salty six" foods identified were:

- Bread and rolls. One piece can have as much as 230 milligrams of sodium.
- Pizza. One slice can contain 760 milligrams of sodium.
- Cold cuts and cured meats. Deli and pre-packaged meats can contain as much as 1,050 milligrams of sodium.

- Poultry. Sodium levels in poultry vary based on how it's prepared. Three ounces of frozen breaded chicken nuggets can have 600 milligrams of sodium.
- Soup. One cup of canned soup can have as much as 940 milligrams of sodium.
- Sandwiches. A sandwich can contain more than the daily recommended amount of sodium.

Most people believe that the excess salt in their diet is due to adding it to food or eating chips and French fries; however, excess salt intake is mostly due to processed and restaurant foods. This excess salt significantly increases cardiovascular risks. It can also cause swelling, and puffiness of the face and under the eyes. A recent study by the American Heart Association found that most Americans take in about 3,400 milligrams of sodium per day. This is well above the recommended upper limit of 2,300 milligrams. The recommended intake is even lower for African Americans, those over age 51, and those with chronic conditions like hypertension, diabetes, and heart disease. Instead of using salt to season your food, try herbs and powders, like garlic powder, onion powder, oregano or basil leaves to name a few.

Heart Healthy Diet

Heart Disease is the number one killer of women. One in three women die every year from heart disease. Heart disease is preventable and starts with eating healthy. On average, a woman needs to consume about 2,000 calories a day to maintain her current weight and 1,500 calories a day to lose one pound per week. This number depends on age, height, activity level, and current weight. There are calorie calculators that can calculate this for you. You should make half of your plate fruits and vegetables and use a smaller plate at meals to help control the amount you eat.

A heart healthy diet consists of:

- Fruits and vegetables. These foods are low in calories and rich in nutrients. They are easy to prepare and convenient for snacking. Keep fruit fresh and washed. You can package them in smaller portions to easily transport to work or access when you are on the go.

- Whole grains provide fiber, which is good for your heart. Examples of whole grains are whole grain bread, oatmeal, high fiber cereal, and brown rice.

- Low-fat dairy, fish, and poultry are great sources of protein. Fish are rich in omega 3 fatty acids, which are good for heart health. Choose low-fat dairy products like skim or 1% milk and low-fat yogurt. Lean meats and skinless chicken are better than fried meats, processed meats, or fatty meats like bacon and ribs.

RENEWING YOUR HEALTH

Get Regular Checkups

Maintaining a healthy body is up to you and is only strengthened by a daily practice of living a healthy lifestyle. This can be achieved by having a relationship with a primary care provider (PCP). Let's first talk about why a relationship with a primary care provider is important. A primary care provider is a physician who knows your history including your family history, medications, allergies, and works on your behalf to coordinate your care. They see the bigger picture by looking at the whole person. Let's say a specialist is treating you for one condition and starts you on a medication. It is important to have a primary care physician who can have this documented with your other medications, cross reference that it is compatible with your current medical condition, and co-manage your health along with your specialist.

Choosing the Right PCP

Choosing the right PCP is important because this is the person who you will hopefully have a relationship with for a long time. It is important that your physician respects your opinions, values, and beliefs. It's also equally important that you respect, listen to, and engage with your primary care physician so that your treatment plan is one that fits your lifestyle and treats your medical condition.

If you do not have a PCP, now is the time to start looking for one. So how do you go about looking for a physician? You can ask for a referral from a family member or friend. They are able to give you the inside scoop about the provider, the provider's office, the hours, etc. Ask your referral source specific questions that you want to know about the provider. Think about what's important to you. You may want to know if the provider takes the time to listen, uses electronic records, communicates electronically, or has convenient office hours.

Regardless of who you choose for your physician you should be honest and forthcoming with information. Withholding information can be dangerous and detrimental to your health. At the end of the day, you and your provider must gel. The only way that a patient-physician relationship can flourish and benefit your health needs is if you both understand your roles, respect one another, communicate effectively, have a level of trust, and you feel comfortable sharing sensitive information.

Taking Time Off for Wellness Visits

Now that you have found your PCP, it's important to schedule time off for your wellness visit. Make your health a priority by scheduling your wellness exam with your provider. As busy women, we sometimes forget to take care of ourselves. A wellness exam is your chance to mention any concerns about your health and to catch health issues before they become a problem. During your visit, your doctor will also ask you about lifestyle behaviors like smoking, excessive alcohol use, sexual health, diet, and exercise. They will also check to make sure your vaccinations, personal, and family history are up to date.

How does one find the time? Here are some tips:

1. **Plan ahead.** Pencil in a date for your wellness exam and let everyone know that you will be unavailable during this time. Giving everyone notice well in advance will likely prevent scheduling conflicts. Also, plan enough time to allow for delays in commute, doctor delays, etc. It's better to get the most out of your visit by not feeling rushed because you arrived late or because an unplanned emergency happened in the doctor's office.

2. **Schedule your wellness visits the same time every year.** Having a consistent time will help you remember to schedule your exam. For example, scheduling around your birthday is a good way to remember.

3. **Ask your company if they have allotted time off for wellness care**. Some companies realize that wellness care is important and reduces absenteeism. If your company does not have allotted time off, plan to use a personal day, schedule your wellness exam on a Saturday morning, or as a last resort schedule an evening appointment.

How to Prepare for Your Visit

When you engage in a health-related visit, what do you want to take away from the encounter or experience? To make sure that you have understood and received the information given, you must be attentive and alert. Get enough sleep the day before so that you are refreshed and ready to receive and ask questions. Ask yourself: "Am I mindfully present?" "Am I free from distractions?" "Am I free from time constraints?

When you are present and mentally focused, you can also engage more fully in your health-related visits and take away a wealth of knowledge and information from the experience. Here are ways to prepare for your visit:

1. **Bring your personal and family medical history or any changes**

    Knowing your family history is important because it is the basis for knowing what you might expect to encounter in your own life. It's also vital information to know so that if there are things that you can do to ward off these diseases, you have the knowledge and tools to begin early. Certain illnesses, like breast cancer, colon cancer and diabetes, can have a genetic link; therefore, if you are aware that these or other illnesses are prevalent in your family, you can start screenings earlier and institute lifestyle changes that may lower your chance of developing these diseases. For example, if there is a family history of breast cancer or colon cancer in your family, your physician may recommend earlier or more frequent screenings. Your physician can also tell you if you are at increased risk of developing a certain type of medical condition.

2. **Bring all your medications including vitamins and herbal medications**

   It's important to bring an updated list of your medications including the dosages. Having the exact information allows the doctor to input this information into your record, which will in turn alert the physician if there are potential interactions between medications. This is also true for herbal medication. Herbal medicines and vitamins can interact with prescription medication. They also have side effects just like prescription medications.

3. **Bring a list of questions and problems you would like to address**
   Come up with a list of questions or health concerns. Maybe you have questions about what you can do to improve your health. Now that you know your family history you may want to discuss risk factors with your physician. Are you at risk for diabetes, heart disease, breast cancer, or colon cancer? Bring a pen and paper or electronic device for documentation. Bring mental clarity and an open mind.

RESTORING YOUR HEALTH

To restore your health, design a business plan for your health goals. First, let's look at how a business plan is designed. A business plan has several parts: Executive Summary, Company Description, Market Analysis, Organization and Management, and Financial Projections. A company that does not have a business plan will not be as successful as one with a plan. The plan is the company's roadmap to success. It keeps the company accountable and allows for changes to be made if a company is not reaching their target.

Your health plan, like a business plan, should be a well thought out document that helps you achieve your goals. If you have developed a health-related S.M.A.R.T.

goal, you can expand on it with this health plan. Grab a journal, paper, or electronic device for documenting.

Your health plan should be organized as follows:

Executive Summary: Here you should list your personal mission statement. Your personal mission statement is an opportunity to clarify and define who you are and what your goals are. Whether it is losing weight, eating healthy, reducing stress, or getting regular checkups, use your values, attributes, and personality to help you achieve those goals. Your personal mission statement should be positive not negative. You want it to give you a sense of purpose. It should only contain your positive attributes and the goals you wish to achieve. Describe here what you want to concentrate on, what success looks like to you, and who you want to become in the area of health and wellness. It should be three to four sentences long.

_____

_____

_____

_____

_____

_____

Company Description: Here, describe who you are, what you do, and what differentiates you from others. For example: age, family history, spiritual connections, hobbies, activities, medical problems, etc.

_____

_____

_____

_____

_____

_____

Market Analysis: This should consist of researching preventive measures, educating yourself about their health risks, and collaborating with your personal physician about treatment options.

_____

_____

_____

_____

_____

_____

Organization and Management: Here consider how your health information is organized. Identify and record your health care providers and keep copies of all important medical documents such as medication list, x-ray reports, mammograms, immunizations, emergency contacts, and health insurance documents.

_____

_____

_____

_____

_____

Health Projections: Where do you see yourself in six months, one year, three years? All business plans have projections to ensure that the defined goals are being met in the proposed time frame. A health plan projection gives you a timeline for reaching health-related goals.

_____

_____

_____

_____

_____

_____

Everyone should want to develop a plan to get healthy because it can increase one's chances of living a long, happy life. So, make a personal health plan for yourself today.

CHAPTER 4:

Achieving Balance in Your Career

The first step to achieving balance in your career is to decide what you want. What is your ideal work environment? What type of career, projects, time off, and salary do you desire? How do you want to use your gifts?

"Balance, peace, and joy are the fruit of a successful life. It starts with recognizing your talents and finding ways to serve others by using them."

—Thomas Kinkade

USE YOUR TALENTS AND GIFTS

Often, your career may not involve work that allows you to use your natural gifts and talents. Your career may not include work that you are passionate about. This lack of passion in your daily activities can lead you to feel disconnected. You may feel that you're not making a difference or contributing to a greater cause. As time goes on, you may begin to resent your work; leading to poor job performance and thoughts about transitioning to a new job or changing careers.

You can change your outlook on your career by deciding what you want. Re-evaluate your current situation at work. If your career is not fueling your passions or using your gifts and talents, how can you change your work environment? One way is to look outside of your immediate surroundings. Are there other projects or teams you can join that include work that interests you? Who can you talk to that will help you find these opportunities? If these projects or ideas don't exist maybe you can create them. Start a new project or bring an idea to your company that would not only benefit them but also feed your interests and passions. People who use their talents and gifts at work are happier, less stressed, and less likely to burnout.

DECIDE ON YOUR LIMITS

Create the space that you need to be able to balance your career and your personal life. Decide what's important for you to have in your life and what you can give up. Taking the time to figure this out allows you to devote your time to the things that matter most. The less important items that you have identified should not be given as much time and attention. This extra time that you have allowed can now be shifted to the important areas.

JOURNALING EXERCISE:

Create a list of the areas in your life that are less important to you. One way to identify what should be categorized as less important is by asking yourself, "If I give it up, will it cause a major shift in my life? Will it affect those close to me?" Then create a list of the things that are less important.

_____

_____

_____

_____

_____

DEVELOP AN IDENTITY OUTSIDE OF WORK

When work takes over our lives, achieving work-life balance becomes difficult. You can no longer focus on the things that bring you joy and peace. If you are constantly playing the same song in your head that work is so consuming, that you don't have time to enjoy the things you like to do, or that you don't have time for family and friends, then you remain locked in the same situation. When you remain stuck, you may miss the opportunity to display your talents in other aspects of your life and live up to your full potential. You need to flip the script and begin to make the changes necessary to find that balance. The feeling of being in balance is life changing. One way to reverse your situation is to develop personal time and find an interest outside of your career. This means taking the time to reflect on what brings you happiness and a sense of purpose. For some, their careers bring them happiness but not a sense of purpose. Others feel like they're making a difference in the world but may not be happy and joyous. Since your career may not give you everything you want, you must find outside interests that can fill those needs. Here are some steps to move you in the direction of developing life outside of work:

Childhood Memories

Think back to your childhood and try to recall what animated you. Some degree of nostalgia is necessary for this level of self-examination. Remember how you felt in your happiest childhood memories and then allow those feelings to surface. Maybe you get a warm, fuzzy feeling inside or butterflies. Maybe you feel a surge of energy that you have not felt in a while. See where this takes you on your journey to exploring new things. If that same or a similar feeling persists after renewing that interest, then you have probably found your answer.

Adult Interests

Maybe something sparked your interest in your adult life that you wish you could continue to do. The good news is you don't have to make it a full-time job. It could be a hobby or a side business. Find ways to incorporate what you love into your schedule.

Try Something New

Try something that you've never done before. I remember spending time with my daughter at a painting event. I don't consider myself to be very artistic, nor had I taken a painting class before; however, I thought it sounded like fun and was willing to give it a try. We attended a painting event and I was pleasantly surprised. I immediately felt relaxed being in an environment with other novice guests. I had to learn to be patient as the guide gave us step-by-step instructions on how to execute the painting using different colors and techniques. I had to give up feeling in control and being a perfectionist. We were told early on that everyone's painting would look different and that no one would win a prize. But the best part was spending time with my daughter and making a connection with her through this event. I found my balance in a painting class, and I encourage you to be brave and curious. Explore activities that you would not normally gravitate toward. And more importantly, have fun!

Volunteer

Give back in your community. Volunteering not only benefits the organization or person whom you are helping, it also helps you, the volunteer. Dr. Martin Luther King Jr. had a legacy of service. He once said, "Life's most persistent and urgent question is, 'What are you doing for others?'"

Volunteering enhances the mind, body, and spirit through physical, mental, and social activities. A few of the many benefits to volunteering include:

- **Increases your social interactions**

Interacting with others can ward off feelings of loneliness, which can often lead to depression. Being in the presence of others who share the same mission can increase your sense of belonging as well as promote relationships, both personal and professional, that can last a lifetime.

- **Provides a level of self-esteem and satisfaction**

Volunteering gives you purpose and helps to develop a personal sense of accomplishment. Often, we may be in careers that are not feeding our ambitions or drive, but through volunteering you can explore your passions, which may guide you to your true purpose.

- **Provides career experience**

Serving on an advisory board or volunteering your skills such as writing, marketing, healthcare, or business development to an organization can enhance your resume and provide you with opportunities that you may not be exposed to on your job.

- **Teaches job skills**

Volunteering teaches transferable skills that can be utilized in nearly any profession. For example, you gain experience working as part of a team, managing your time, coordinating projects and programs, and speaking publicly.

- **Provides health benefits**

There are many health benefits to volunteering as well. Volunteering leads to increased physical activity, which is good for your heart and blood pressure. According to the American Psychological Association, those who volunteered at least 200 hours in one year had a lowered risk of developing hypertension than those who did not volunteer. It can also reduce stress by providing positive feelings when helping others. The feeling of contributing your time and talents to make someone's future brighter can replace stress and worry and bring joy and happiness into your life.

Where will you find balance? What will you commit to trying?

DEVELOP A SCHEDULE

Create a schedule to achieve balance in your personal life. Stay organized with a to-do list or calendar that allows you to list your tasks for the day. This frees your mind from having to remember every detail and allows you to check off tasks as they are completed. It is impossible to try to do everything and make everyone happy. Don't get overwhelmed with the feeling that you have to check off every task by the end of the day. Develop a list of things that are the most important to you and successfully complete those events. Choose the tasks first that will bring you the greatest return. It's better to do less and be more efficient with less stress, than to do more with a great deal of stress and inefficiency. By prioritizing your tasks, it reduces your chances of becoming overwhelmed. You can begin to act and make progress based on a well thought out plan. Your plan should consist of tackling the most important, high priority tasks first.

Once these tasks are completed, you can then move to the less important, low impact tasks. Don't use your calendar only for tasks and projects; also use it to schedule time for exercise, children's activities, dates with friends, or any event that is important to you. If you are committed to exercising three times a week for 30 minutes, look at your calendar and pencil in the time. Now you have an appointment for exercise and will plan accordingly. Putting it on the calendar means that you are committed to making time for the activity. It also allows you to be able to say no to other things that might interfere with your scheduled activities.

JOURNALING EXERCISE:

Create a list of the activities in your childhood that made you happy and you would like to revisit.

_____

_____

_____

_____

_____

What new event or activity would you like to try? List five ideas:

_____

_____

_____

_____

_____

What organization would you like to volunteer with? What areas are you passionate about giving back to? Where can your talents and gifts be useful?

_____

_____

_____

_____

_____

CHAPTER 5:

How to Have Balance in Your Relationships

"It's all about quality of life and finding a happy balance between work and friends and family."

—Philip Green

PARENTING

How Busy Moms Can Stay Connected to Their Children

- **Stop the guilt**

"There is no decision that we can make that doesn't come with some sort of balance or sacrifice."

—Simon Sinek

As moms, we are faced with making decisions daily that affect our families. We are not given a handbook on how to raise children. Instead, we often adopt behaviors based on how we were raised and what we experienced in our own lives. We learn to adapt and change our approach based on trial and error. Sometimes our decisions are not ones that our children are happy with; however, we know as parents that it is in their best interest. Nevertheless, denying them often starts to invoke a feeling of guilt in us. Guilt arises when you feel bad about a situation that you internalize as having done incorrectly or when you failed to meet a commitment to someone or something. As moms, we want to make everyone happy, especially our children. We want them to have more opportunities than we had and grow up with everything they need. Somehow, we feel that if this is not accomplished, we have failed our children and let them down. What we need to realize is that as long as we try our best and have our children's best interest at heart, we have done enough. Moms are obligated to make sure their children are cared for with love, food, clothing, and shelter. We are obligated to make sure that our children are protected. We are obligated to help our children become the best human beings they can be. We are also responsible for teaching them right from wrong, empathy, and how to be kind and respectful to others. For these reasons, we often sacrifice our own wants and needs for those of our children. We go *without* to make sure our children *have*.

As working moms, guilt often arises from pressure that we put on ourselves. We feel that by working, we deprive our children of our time. We feel that this lack of time spent with our children will adversely affect them and they will grow up feeling neglected. Our other fear is that they will become angry with us. We hold on to the guilt that we have done something wrong by deciding to have a career and work. However, most studies show that a stable home life is more important than whether or not a mom works. What is important is that mothers are committed to their child's development and can provide stability.

- **Make the time spent meaningful**

What we must realize as working moms is that the time we spend with our children should be meaningful. We must make a concerted effort to carve out time to connect with our children and to show them how important and special they are. It's the quality of the time spent and not the quantity. Spending quality time means giving the child in your presence undivided attention. Our children just want us to be present when we're with them. Being present means putting down your electronic devices. This is difficult for some of us, as our electronic devices have become our lifeline. Our devices provide easy and direct accessibility. A simple text or email will come across our screen in seconds and our first reaction is to respond. Responding to a text or email while spending time with our children takes away from the feeling of importance that our children are looking for. They want to feel more important than the text you are responding to. Spending quality time can also be achieved by listening instead of responding. Our children want to be heard, especially pre-teens and teenagers. They want our undivided attention from the beginning of their talk to the end. They also want to be understood. The best way to acknowledge that you understand your child is to repeat back to them what you heard and clarify what they mean. During this time of conversation, giving eye contact and not taking on another task at the same time also shows that you are committed to communicating in a way that allows your child to share his or her feelings. Try to just listen and not solve their problems. Try to serve as a resource and a confidant.

- **Connect during mealtime**

Mealtime is a crucial time of the day to connect with your children. As busy families, mealtime often happens on the road and is not spent together; however, breakfast or dinner can be a time to catch up on what's happening in your child's life, to reconnect with stories or shared memories, and to discuss events happening in the world.

Talking during mealtime helps your child learn how to express themselves verbally. To raise socially conscious, compassionate children we have to talk about the circumstances of others and how we can contribute to the development of a society where we all are each other's keeper. I know that having every meal together may be tough, especially as children get older and are involved in activities, but setting aside three to four days a week that is designated as family mealtime goes a long way. The best way to achieve this is to plan. Look at everyone's schedule and see what days and times work best. Also, include the children in the decision-making process. Ask them what foods they would like to have. Not only will family mealtime help to deepen your relationship, but per a new review of previous research, an article by Rutgers University also discovered that families who regularly eat together during mealtime were healthier. They also have a lower body mass index and kids eat more fruits, vegetables and nutrient rich foods. Don't let mealtime be a stressful event, plan and involve the entire family.

- **Create memories**

Leaving behind heartfelt messages for your children is a way to connect and to let them know that you're thinking about them. These acts are not only for couples. They can be shared and extended to parents and their children.

An example of these messages is sending texts after they get on the school bus or after they leave your car if you're dropping them off. Leaving notes in their lunchbox is also a pleasant surprise and can brighten their day, especially if your child is having a hard time adjusting. You can also leave encouraging notes on the refrigerator. This is the one place they are sure to visit. I would often leave inspirational notes for my son before a basketball game or good luck notes for my children when it was test time or they were trying out for a team. Also, try creating memories during the holidays, birthdays, or during the summer when they are out of school. This not only gives them something to look forward to every year, but also creates special impressions that will last a lifetime.

- **Be an example for self-care**

When we practice self-care, we teach our children, especially our daughters, to do the same. Women are by nature caregivers, problem solvers, and nurturers. We carry the weight for the whole team. These characteristics can lead to feelings of stress and burnout if we take on too much and push ourselves too hard. Stress can lead to poor relationships with our children. We can start to feel disconnected, become irritable and impatient, and make our children feel neglected. Sometimes, stress cannot be avoided but it *can* be managed. To help manage stress, we must remember to take time to recharge and feed our souls. This in turn will allow us to give to others freely and without resentment or guilt.

MARRIAGE BALANCE

"The best thing to hold onto in life is each other."

—Audrey Hepburn

We all know how hard it is to balance work and home and to also have a healthy, vibrant marriage. True love in a marriage makes you feel good. It's forgiving, non-judgmental, supportive, and resilient. Responsibilities of both spouses can interfere with one-on-one time, the ability to reconnect, and the ease of communication. It's important to keep the lines of communication open to maintain a healthy marriage. It's also important to spend quality time with one another. Having balance in your marriage requires practicing habits that will make your union successful.

- **Be present**

Don't let other things get in the way. Schedule one-on-one time and make sure everyone knows that this time is scheduled and you will not allow interruptions.

By planning time alone, you are showing your spouse how important it is to you to have time to connect. You are showing him that you value your relationship and are willing to devote time to your growth as a couple. During this time, make sure to turn off all interruptions. In this digital age, it is difficult to disconnect; so, make a concerted effort to turn off electronic devices. You want your spouse to have your full attention.

- **Listen**

To listen is to pay attention fully. To fully pay attention, we must not be involved in other activities. When engaged in conversation, let your spouse finish so that they know they are heard and understood. If you are unclear about any part of the conversation, repeat what you heard and let your partner clarify. Don't answer until you clearly understand what was said. Allow your spouse to speak without judgment. Let your spouse know you heard them and that you understand what they want and need.

- **Communicate effectively**

Having effective communication is key to having a balanced, healthy relationship. Some people are better communicators than others. A person's communication style stems from previous experiences. For instance, a person who grew up in a household where communication was poor, expressing yourself was shunned, or verbal abuse was experienced will often shut down. We need to recognize these barriers in ourselves and our partners, and try to communicate better by asking for and providing an environment that is supportive and open. When communicating, we must not only watch what we say but how we say it. Certain gestures and body language can give the impression that you are not interested, or that you are frustrated with the other person's comments. When communicating, make sure you get your point across clearly. Don't assume that your spouse knows what you want if you have not effectively communicated it. When communicating, also be willing to admit when you're wrong. Accept responsibility and be willing to forgive your partner if they have said something that was hurtful.

- **Be supportive**

Give positive comments freely. Everyone likes to receive uplifting words. Not only do uplifting words make the person feel good, but they also show that you are thinking about them and appreciate them. The next time your spouse does something without you asking, recognize it and let him know. Notice when he wears a new outfit, gets a haircut, or puts on the cologne you like. Just as women like to receive gifts, men also like to receive random thoughts of kindness.

Recognize your spouse's strengths and gifts. Maybe there is a thing that they do exceptionally well. Let them know that you appreciate the fact that they are a good provider or that you value the contributions that they make to the household.

In addition to being supportive, it's ok to ask for support as well. If you have a demanding career or own a business, you know how important it is to have a partner who supports you; so, if there is a way that your spouse can be there for you, ask for it. What does that look like? Maybe it's contributing more to household chores so you can have extra time to devote to your work. Would it be beneficial if he helped with picking up the kids, laundry, or cleaning? Decide as a couple what arrangements work best. Be specific.

- **Connect with couples who have healthy marriages**

Connect with other couples who have long-lasting, healthy marriages. Use their insights, experiences, and wisdom on how they managed to have a successful marriage to improve your own. Let them be your support system. Marriages are likely to last if you and your spouse have mentors in marriage. Sometimes just hearing how another person overcame obstacles or dealt with challenges can give you the needed boost to bounce back and work your way through it. Reach out to other couples and arrange for date nights or a fun outing like bowling.

- **Create memories**

Create memories as a couple. Memories are created when you take the time to be in each other's presence and commit to being in the moment. What extra effort can be put in to make sure your time spent together is special and etched in your memory forever? Create the scene you would like to have. It can be as simple as taking time to walk on the beach together, having dinner in a romantic setting, or planning a dream vacation and taking time to celebrate anniversaries and accomplishments. You can also participate in an activity that you are both passionate about and could bring you closer together.

NURTURE YOUR FRIENDSHIPS

As working moms, friendships can get lost in the constant rush of our busy lives. Long work hours, raising a family, and trying to squeeze in some 'me time,' can cause us to become inattentive to our relationships with our friends. The journey for some of us involved getting married, having children, then embarking on our careers. This changed the way we lived our lives. For some of us, moving to a different location made it difficult to sustain the close relationships we once had with our friends. It also brought on the new and scary challenge of trying to get to know new people and establish new friendships.

As we age, it's just as important to maintain those friendships we had in our 20's. Our lives begin to take on new challenges like marriage, divorce, children, aging parents, and career transitions. Having someone in your corner to support you through these changes can make all the difference. There are many benefits to sustaining friendships. A few are as follows:

- **Acceptance**

Sometimes we can feel like we are not accepted. By taking time off from work to care for our families, we can be perceived as not putting in as much time as our coworkers. We can also be perceived by non-working moms as not spending enough time with our kids, which can lead to a feeling of unacceptance. Knowing that we have friends who accept us for who we are, boosts our self-confidence and reduces our stress and anxiety about the choices we make as moms.

- **Support**

We need support to be successful at work and at home. Our girlfriends, who are our sisters, mothers, aunties, college buddies, and coworkers, are the women who help us celebrate the good times and support us during the tough times. Support from friends can be in the form of making a phone call, offering help with childcare, lending a listening ear, or offering a shoulder to cry on.

- **Balance**

Being able to take time off to spend with friends and just have fun can give us the boost we need to push through our daily encounters. The meaningful, interpersonal bond we have with friends helps us to live healthier, more balanced lives.

If you want to restore balance to your life, nurture your relationship with your friends. Close your eyes and think back to when you were younger. Can you remember that carefree feeling you felt when you and your girlfriends were hanging out together? Let the nostalgia take over. Once it seeps in, work to recreate that feeling and rebuild that bond that you and your friends once had. Here are some ways to nurture your friendships:

- **Reconnect with an old friend**

Reconnecting with friends is good for the mind, body, and soul. Is there an old friend, who often comes up in conversation, that you miss talking to or hanging out with? Reach out to an old friend that you have not heard from recently. After you make the first contact, see where the conversation and the relationship take you. Be patient, it takes time to build friendships.

- **Support a friend**

There is nothing like the support of a friend, who shows up when least expected. Sometimes we are not as pro-active about supporting each other because of distance or time. As women, it's important that we support each other. Support may come in the form of helping a friend who just suffered a loss or is going through an illness. It can also be supporting a friend's business or dream. Even if you don't share the same interest as your friend's business, you can provide support by sending a note or card letting her know how proud you are of her. You can refer others you may know who have the same interests or need her services. Lending support strengthens your bond and your friend will provide the same support for you when needed.

- **Forgive a friend**

Forgiveness is essential to our emotional well-being. Carrying around anger and resentment can lead to stress, anxiety, depression, and chronic illnesses. Forgiveness is not about condoning the behavior, but about freeing yourself from the toxic feelings you harbor and allowing joy into your life. Know that one wrong deed by a person does not dampen your ability to establish long- lasting relationships with others. Renew your faith in friendship. Be willing to be open and flexible. If we stick our heads in the sand and dig our toes deep in the ground, we will never open up to the possibility of what forgiveness can do for our mind, body, and soul. It takes a lot of strength to forgive someone who has hurt you.

- **Plan a girls' night out**

Spending quality time together is important for maintaining long-lasting friendships because it allows us to detach from the stresses of our everyday lives. Spending time with friends has been shown to decrease stress and improve your mood. So, set an appointment for spending time with your bestie and make this time just as important as your other dates. Make your friend feel special and worthy of your time.

Decide what fun activity you both would like to do. Here are some examples:

- Spa day
- Movie night
- Night out dancing
- Dinner
- Concert

CHAPTER 6:

How to Achieve a Healthy Mental Balance

"Mental health includes our emotional, psychological, and social well-being. It affects how we think, feel, and act. It also helps determine how we handle stress, relate to others, and make choices. Mental health is important at every stage of life, from childhood and adolescence through adulthood."

—MentalHealth.gov

Achieving a healthy mental balance is important because it allows you to live a fulfilled life. It allows you to be your best self in your relationships and your connection with others. With a healthy mental balance, you can give freely and openly without feeling stressed. You can nurture your creativity and more easily adapt to change. Our mental balance can begin to shift when we allow stressors to take over our lives. When we develop chronic stress from work, responsibilities at home, poor finances, or traumatic experiences our mental balance can begin to suffer. Approximately 12 million women in the U.S. experience clinical depression each year. Women of all races, religions, and ages can develop depression.

Depression can be caused by genetics, hormonal shifts, or other factors such as having a child or experiencing menopause.

"Being in control of your life and having realistic expectations about your day-to-day challenges are the keys to stress management, which is perhaps the most important ingredient to living a happy, healthy and rewarding life."

—Marilu Henner

WHAT IS STRESS?

Stress is your body's response to a change that is occurring. The change is usually perceived as something you have no control over. The change can be due to external stressors or internal factors. The external stressors can be categorized into good stress or bad stress. Examples of good stress include: buying a home, sending a child off to college, or getting a promotion. Bad stress, on the other hand, could be caused by financial strain, going through a divorce, or the death of a loved one. There are also the day-to-day pressures of work, family, and other daily responsibilities.

Our body reacts to this stress with a natural fight or flight response that releases the hormones adrenaline and cortisol. Adrenaline increases your heart rate, elevates your blood pressure, and boosts your energy supplies. Cortisol increases sugars in the bloodstream, and curbs functions that would be nonessential or detrimental in a fight or flight response. In addition, cortisol is known to alter immune responses. This natural response is good in the case of an emergency such as getting away from danger; however, if the response goes on for too long, which happens in the case of chronic stress, it can cause physical symptoms. Nearly *four in five* adults regularly experience physical symptoms associated with stress. Studies also show that women are more likely to experience physical symptoms of stress than men. Some examples of physical symptoms of stress include fatigue, palpitations, jitteriness, muscle aches, abdominal pain, or headaches. These symptoms can lead to health issues like high blood pressure, depression, anxiety, and increase your risk for heart disease and diabetes.

When you are dealing with stress do you?

- Drink alcohol or smoke to stay calm
- Eat more
- Sleep too much or too little
- Feel fatigued mentally and physically
- Procrastinate

If you answered yes to any of the above, it may mean that you are not dealing with stress effectively. To manage stress, we must change how we react to it by modifying our behavior and lifestyle choices. This can be accomplished by following these **FIVE STRESS TIPS:**

1. UNDERSTAND HOW YOU STRESS

    To understand how stress manifests itself in your life you have to start paying close attention to what's going on around you. You need to start developing a sense of how you feel when faced with challenges. What is the first thing that you do? Do you start with negative thinking? Do you withdraw? Do you start to question everything? Keeping a journal of what's happening with your mood and your attitude will help you not only understand how stress shows up in your life, but it will also allow you to be aware of these changes and respond with a more positive outlook.

2. IDENTIFY YOUR SOURCES OF STRESS

    What causes you stress? For some, it's work demands, world events, holidays, financial stress, or home responsibilities. You should be able to easily identify what causes you stress because exposure to these areas of your life will usually elicit that fight or flight response mentioned above.

You may start to get sweaty palms or feel anxious. Your stomach may start to hurt or your neck may begin to stiffen. Once you identify your source of stress, you can work on ways to respond to the situation. Instead of letting your stress affect you physically, take a couple of deep breaths or count to ten. If you start to feel anxious at work, get up and walk away from your desk or the situation to calm down. We often cannot escape stressful situations, but we can change how we respond to them.

3. LEARN YOUR OWN STRESS SIGNALS

    How do you feel when you are stressed? What are some early warning signs that can alert you to the fact that something or someone is causing you stress? Do you become angry, irritable, or tense up? If these are some of your early warning signals, pay attention to when they occur and then try to figure out the root cause.

4. FIND HEALTHY WAYS TO MANAGE STRESS

    Managing stress is a process that takes time to develop. In the beginning, you may find yourself reverting to your old ways, but like anything else you must keep at it until it becomes a habit. Instead of unhealthy behaviors like consuming more alcohol, eating more, or sleeping too much or too little, you should work on healthy responses like trying to get plenty of sleep, exercising, and taking breaks.

Preparation

If we better prepare ourselves, we can manage stress more effectively. Here are some preparation tips:

- Keep a calendar of important events - personal and professional.
- Take large projects or tasks and break them down into smaller more achievable tasks.
- Prepare for life events such as an aging parent, job loss, health issues, financial security, or children.
- Disconnect from social media and other media outlets when needed.

Quick stress relievers

- Count to ten before you go into a meeting or speak to someone
- Take three to five deep breaths
- Take a walk or walk away from a stressful situation
- Hug a loved one
- Write in a gratitude journal

- Pray
- Set your watch five to ten minutes ahead to avoid being late

Find pleasurable activities

- Delve into a new hobby
- Listen to music
- Hang out with friends
- Read an enjoyable book or magazine

Self-Talk

We all have thoughts in our head that we can start to believe as truth if we do not recognize the source. Negative self-talk increases stress. Positive self-statements are one way to deal with stress. If we put into the world positive thinking, we will get that in return. Positive thinking forces us to have realistic expectations. This entails reframing your thoughts and changing the way you look at things. Positive thinking is looking at situations with the glass half full instead of half empty. We begin to look for the opportunities in challenges. Replacing negative statements with positive statements takes time and practice. When practiced consistently, our productivity improves as well as our outlook and responses to challenging situations.

Examples of positive responses to help alleviate stress:

Negative statement: "I can't get all this work done."
Positive response: "I'll get as much done as I can."

Negative statement: "I let my family down."
Positive response: "We all make mistakes. I'm human."

Negative statement: "I'll never get back to my old weight again."

Positive response: "If I take my time and work toward my goals, I'll be successful."

Healthy stress-reducing diet

A healthy diet can positively impact the negative effects of stress. Here are some useful tips to keep in mind:

- Decrease or discontinue caffeine, eat a protein rich breakfast every morning, and consume more fruits, vegetables, cereals, and nuts.
- Complex carbs prompt the brain to make more serotonin - a hormone that induces happiness.
- Examples: whole grain breads, pasta, cereals
- Oranges contain vitamin C, which reduces stress level hormones and strengthens the immune system.

- Spinach provides magnesium, which is helpful with fatigue and headaches. Soybeans and salmon are also high in magnesium.
- Omega 3 fatty acids found in salmon and tuna prevents surges in stress hormones.
- Nuts, like pistachios, walnuts and almonds, lower cholesterol, reduce diabetes, and ease inflammation in heart arteries. Almonds also have Vitamins E and B, which help the immune system.

5. RECONNECT WITH YOUR SPIRITUALITY
Reclaim your health by reconnecting spiritually. Being connected spiritually brings renewed energy, it strengthens your mind-body-spirit connection, and it provides you with an overall sense of well-being. You can stay connected to your spirit by practicing the following:

Meditation

Meditation allows you to experience more compassion, remove the clutter from your brain, and connect to your feelings. Just five minutes can get you on your way to a life of bliss and fulfillment.

Some benefits of meditation are:

- Improvement in concentration and focus. When we are trying to balance work and life, meditation can provide the clarity we need.

- Improvement of health by lowering blood pressure, reducing risk of heart disease.
- Improvement in mood. Meditation has been shown to improve your mood and reduce anxiety and depression.
- Reduction in stress. By focusing on your breathing and blocking out all the negative thought and worries, your stress level will in turn lower.

So how does one meditate? It does not have to be complicated. Meditation should take place in a quiet room where you are less likely to be distracted. Pick a posture that works for you. Sitting on the floor with your legs crossed, lying down, or sitting in a chair are all acceptable. Next, close your eyes. Then, take deep breaths in and out and focus on your breathing. Breathe naturally. If your mind wanders just bring your focus back to your breathing. With consistent meditation, you will find that your mind will wander less. Don't try to meditate for a long time, start with just five to ten minutes and gradually increase your time.

Walking/Quiet Time

Not only can walking serve as a form of exercise, but it will also allow you to have some quiet time to connect with nature and your inner thoughts. It gives you time to reflect on your goals and dreams.

Gratitude

When gratitude becomes your habit, spiritual well-being becomes your lifestyle. Keeping a gratitude journal is a wonderful way to remember all that we should be thankful for. Practicing gratitude improves sleep, lowers stress, and improves your mood. Consistent journaling can change the way we think about certain situations. By concentrating on the positive events in our lives, we begin to concentrate less on what we don't have. Being grateful allows you to connect with others at a higher level. This can be thought of as a spiritual connection.

Take Time Off

Learning to take the time to recoup in between challenging times is also important. Time is needed to recharge so that it's easier to be resilient and bounce back. Take time for yourself. A study by Oxford Economics revealed that many U.S. workers do not use all their allotted vacation time. More than four out of ten employees finished 2013 with unused P.T.O. Those unused vacation days can have a negative effect on employees and companies. A vacation gives you the opportunity to de-stress, disconnect and recharge. Per Oxford Economics' research, employees report returning to work feeling renewed, refreshed, and ready to work. Even batteries have a time limit on how long they will provide energy before running out. A vacation can be an extended time off like one to two weeks, a mini-vacation for two to three days, or even a staycation can do the trick. A vacation should be planned so that you can tighten up any loose ends, work responsibilities can be shifted to others, and everyone is aware in advance of your time away. This will lessen the feeling of guilt from taking time off. Everyone needs a time out, so begin planning yours and continue to do so every year.

Conclusion

I hope that after reading this book you have uncovered your reason for seeking work-life balance.

What does work-life balance mean to you?

Only you can answer this question. Your response is not going to be like anyone else's response. Your understanding of work-life balance is individual and depends on your current situation, circumstances, and experiences. Now that you have completed this book, you should be able to visualize what balance looks and feels like to you. Are you working less hours, in a different department? Do you have time for family functions? What hobbies or volunteer activities would you like to incorporate into your schedule? What will it feel like? Will you have less stress? Will you feel like you found your motivation again? Will you feel empowered? What will making these changes do for you? Now that you know what balance looks like, don't hold back. Think big. Create this vision and write it down on paper. Keep it in an area where you can see it daily and reflect upon what you are aiming for.

Why is having work-life balance important?

If after reading this book you discovered why balance is important for you, that discovery will keep you motivated. Your goal will now be tied to the outcome you are looking for. Is work-life balance important because you want to enjoy your work? Is it because spending time with family is important to you? Maybe you have young children and you don't want to miss any milestones. Is having work-life balance important for your health? What were the reasons you discovered and how will this take priority in your life?

Where in your life is lack of work-life balance showing up?

Are you having trouble sleeping at night because your work is causing you stress? Have you gained a few extra pounds because you don't have time to exercise? Are you having strained relationships? What are the areas of your life that are being neglected or require improvements?

Who can help you?

Who did you identify as your village? Who can help you improve the balance between working and your personal life? Who can call on for assistance? What are their roles? Now that you have identified the people who can support you and identified their roles, you have a clearer idea of who you can call on in times of need and for what purpose. If there are areas of your life where you are lacking support, who can provide it?

When are you going to put your action plan into place?

Having a timeline helps to make sure that your goals are achieved and your actions are accounted for. Now that you have identified what your ideal life would look like, why it's important, where you need to make changes, and who can help you, it's time to sit down and map out an action plan. Enjoy the journey!

References

Elliott, A.M. *Working hours around the world: Does work-life balance exist?* www.mashable.com.

4/27/2015-June 2014. *Nine Facts About American Families and Work.* White House report.

Harris Poll on behalf of Ernest and Young Global Limited, within the United States between November 20, 2014, and January 14, 2015, among 9,699 adults aged 18–67.

Pedersen, T. *Moms in Medicine Can Benefit from Support Groups at Work.* Study at Arizona State University (ASU) and the Mayo Clinic showed that these caregiving women can significantly reduce their feelings of burnout by participating in support groups at work.

Prochaska and DiClemente. *The Stages of Change Model.*

New York Times "Well" report: Exercise may improve memory and the ability to perform skilled tasks by increasing production of a protein that stimulates nerve cell health. Studies also indicate that there may be a benefit of exercise in reducing the risk of breast cancer.

Hildebrand, MPH, J. October 4, 2013. *Recreational Physical Activity and Leisure-Time Sitting in Relation to Postmenopausal Breast Cancer Risk - Cancer Epidemiology, Biomarkers, and Prevention.* American Cancer Society.

Morgan, Dr. M.H., DTR, K.T. *Family Mealtimes – Making it a Priority.* Rutgers New Jersey Agricultural Experiment Station.

What is Mental Health? www.mentalhealth.gov.

Depression in Women. 1999. National Institute of Mental Health, Unpublished Epidemiological Catchment Area Analyses. www.mentalhealthamerica.net.

Gender and Stress. American Psychological Association. www.apa.org.

Oxford Economics - An assessment of paid time off in the US: Implications for employees, companies and the economy. February 2014.

Dr. Lisa Herbert

The Salty Six Surprising Foods That Add the Most Sodium to Our Diets. American Heart Association. www.sodiumbreakup.heart.org.

About the Author

Dr. Lisa Herbert, "The Balance Doctor," is a family doctor, certified professional coach, and the Founder and CEO of Just the Right Balance, LLC™. After graduating from Stony Brook University, Dr. Herbert received her medical degree from Upstate Medical Center, concluded her residency in Family Medicine at Mountainside Hospital, and completed her training as a Certified Personal and Executive Coach with The Coaching Institute of Applied Positive Psychology.

As a family physician serving the community for 22 years, Dr. Herbert has held the position of Clinical Assistant Professor in the Department of Family Medicine at the University of Medicine and Dentistry of

New Jersey, and received the Degree of Fellow from the American Academy of Family Physicians.

Dr. Herbert is a wife and proud mother of two. When she is not working, she achieves balance by enjoying the arts, traveling, reading an enjoyable book, and spending time with family.

To connect, visit her website at
www.justtherightbalance.com

TO SCHEDULE SPEAKING ENGAGEMENTS OR WORKSHOPS

Contact me at

info@justtherightbalance.com

IF YOU'RE A WORKING MOM READY TO TAKE BACK YOUR LIFE AND REDEFINE WORK-LIFE BALANCE ON YOUR OWN TERMS

Join a community of like-minded women in our Working Mom Redefined Group Coaching Program. Sign up at http://www.justtherightbalance.com/working-moms.html

For more information, visit

www.justtherightbalance.com

Connect on social media

Twitter: @thebalancedr

Facebook: JusttheRightBalance

Instagram: JusttheRightBalance

CREATING DISTINCTIVE BOOKS WITH INTENTIONAL RESULTS

We're a collaborative group of creative masterminds with a mission to produce high-quality books to position you for monumental success in the marketplace.

Our professional team of writers, editors, designers, and marketing strategists work closely together to ensure that every detail of your book is a clear representation of the message in your writing.

Want to know more?
Write to us at info@publishyourgift.com
or call (888) 949-6228

Discover great books, exclusive offers, and more at
www.PublishYourGift.com

Connect with us on social media

@publishyourgift

www.ingramcontent.com/pod-product-compliance
Lightning Source LLC
Chambersburg PA
CBHW071525080526
44588CB00011B/1559